SELECTED POEMS OF
JAMES HOGG

SELECTED POEMS OF JAMES HOGG

EDITED BY

J. W. OLIVER

PUBLISHED FOR

THE SALTIRE SOCIETY

BY

OLIVER AND BOYD LTD

1940

PRINTED IN GREAT BRITAIN BY
OLIVER AND BOYD LTD., EDINBURGH

PREFACE

It is difficult, within the limits of a small volume such as this, to make an adequate selection from a poet who wrote so much as Hogg, and—despite his frequent lapses and failures to bring ambitious things off—so much that is really good. I have tried, as far as possible, to make the selection representative. His longer poems are represented by the obvious choices, *Kilmeny* and *The Witch of Fife*, and I have given them in full. There is much to be said for abridging *Kilmeny*; but Hogg evidently thought differently and it seems only fair to allow it to stand as he wrote it, and not as a group of unrelated purple patches. I have also included *The Flying Tailor*, the Wordsworthian parody from *The Poetic Mirror*, as an example of what this untaught shepherd could do in the highly sophisticated art of parody. *The Mermaid* and *The Witch's Chant* are specimens, shorter than *Kilmeny* and *The Witch of Fife*, of that glamourie and diablerie in which Hogg excelled. The rest of the book, with the exception of the closing stanzas from *The Queen's Wake*, consists of songs.

The text of the songs has been taken from the 1831 collection of them, that of the other poems from the 1822 collected edition of the poetical works and—for a few works not included in that collection—from the Centenary Edition of 1874.

KILMENY

BONNY Kilmeny gaed up the glen ;
But it wasna to meet Duneira's men,
Nor the rosy monk of the isle to see,
For Kilmeny was pure as pure could be.
It was only to hear the Yorlin sing,
And pu' the cress-flower round the spring ;
The scarlet hypp and the hindberrye,
And the nut that hang frae the hazel tree ;
For Kilmeny was pure as pure could be.
But lang may her minny look o'er the wa',
And lang may she seek i' the green-wood shaw ;
Lang the laird of Duneira blame,
And lang, lang greet or Kilmeny come hame !

When many a day had come and fled,
When grief grew calm, and hope was dead,
When mess for Kilmeny's soul had been sung,
When the bedes-man had prayed, and the dead bell
    rung,
Late, late in a gloamin when all was still,
When the fringe was red on the westlin hill,
The wood was sere, the moon i' the wane,
The reek o' the cot hung over the plain,
Like a little wee cloud in the world its lane ;
When the ingle lowed with an eiry leme,
Late, late in the gloamin Kilmeny came hame !

" Kilmeny, Kilmeny, where have you been ?
Lang hae we sought baith holt and den ;
By linn, by ford, and green-wood tree,
Yet you are halesome and fair to see.

Where gat you that joup o' the lily scheen ?
That bonny snood of the birk sae green ?
And these roses, the fairest that ever were seen ?
Kilmeny, Kilmeny, where have you been ? "

Kilmeny looked up with a lovely grace,
But nae smile was seen on Kilmeny's face ;
As still was her look, and as still was her ee,
As the stillness that lay on the emerant lea,
Or the mist that sleeps on a waveless sea.
For Kilmeny had been she knew not where,
And Kilmeny had seen what she could not declare ;
Kilmeny had been where the cock never crew,
Where the rain never fell, and the wind never blew ;
But it seemed as the harp of the sky had rung,
And the airs of heaven played round her tongue,
When she spake of the lovely forms she had seen,
And a land where sin had never been ;
A land of love, and a land of light,
Withouten sun, or moon, or night ;
Where the river swa'd a living stream,
And the light a pure celestial beam :
The land of vision it would seem,
A still, an everlasting dream.

In yon green-wood there is a waik,
And in that waik there is a wene,
And in that wene there is a maike,
That neither has flesh, blood, nor bane ;
And down in yon green-wood he walks his lane.

In that green wene Kilmeny lay,
Her bosom happed wi' the flowerets gay ;
But the air was soft and the silence deep,
And bonny Kilmeny fell sound asleep.
She kend nae mair, nor opened her ee,
Till waked by the hymns of a far countrye.

She 'wakened on a couch of the silk sae slim,
All striped wi' the bars of the rainbow's rim ;
And lovely beings round were rife,
Who erst had travelled mortal life ;
And aye they smiled, and 'gan to speer,
" What spirit has brought this mortal here ? "

" Lang have I journeyed the world wide,"
A meek and reverend fere replied ;
" Baith night and day I have watched the fair,
Eident a thousand years and mair.
Yes, I have watched o'er ilk degree,
Wherever blooms femenitye ;
But sinless virgin, free of stain
In mind and body, fand I nane.
Never, since the banquet of time,
Found I a virgin in her prime,
Till late this bonny maiden I saw
As spotless as the morning snaw :
Full twenty years she has lived as free
As the spirits that sojourn this countrye :
I have brought her away frae the snares of men,
That sin or death she never may ken."

They clasped her waist and her hands sae fair,
They kissed her cheek, and they kemed her hair,
And round came many a blooming fere,
Saying, " Bonny Kilmeny, ye're welcome here !
Women are freed of the littand scorn :
O, blessed be the day Kilmeny was born !
Now shall the land of the spirits see,
Now shall it ken what a woman may be !
Many a lang year in sorrow and pain,
Many a lang year through the world we've gane,
Commissioned to watch fair womankind,
For it's they who nurice the immortal mind.

We have watched their steps as the dawning shone,
And deep in the green-wood walks alone ;
By lily bower and silken bed,
The viewless tears have o'er them shed ;
Have soothed their ardent minds to sleep,
Or left the couch of love to weep.
We have seen ! we have seen ! but the time must come,
And the angels will weep at the day of doom !

" O, would the fairest of mortal kind
Aye keep the holy truths in mind,
That kindred spirits their motions see,
Who watch their ways with anxious ee,
And grieve for the guilt of humanitye !
O, sweet to Heaven the maiden's prayer,
And the sigh that heaves a bosom sae fair !
And dear to Heaven the words of truth,
And the praise of virtue frae beauty's mouth !
And dear to the viewless forms of air,
The minds that kyth as the body fair !

" O, bonny Kilmeny ! free frae stain,
If ever you seek the world again,
That world of sin, of sorrow and fear,
O, tell of the joys that are waiting here ;
And tell of the signs you shall shortly see ;
Of the times that are now, and the times that shall be."

They lifted Kilmeny, they led her away,
And she walked in the light of a sunless day :
The sky was a dome of crystal bright,
The fountain of vision, and fountain of light :
The emerald fields were of dazzling glow,
And the flowers of everlasting blow.
Then deep in the stream her body they laid,
That her youth and beauty never might fade ;

And they smiled on heaven, when they saw her lie
In the stream of life that wandered bye.
And she heard a song, she heard it sung,
She kend not where ; but sae sweetly it rung,
It fell on her ear like a dream of the morn :
" O ! blest be the day Kilmeny was born !
Now shall the land of the spirits see,
Now shall it ken what a woman may be !
The sun that shines on the world sae bright,
A borrowed gleid frae the fountain of light ;
And the moon that sleeks the sky sae dun,
Like a gouden bow, or a beamless sun,
Shall wear away, and be seen nae mair,
And the angels shall miss them travelling the air.
But lang, lang after baith night and day,
When the sun and the world have elyed away ;
When the sinner has gane to his waesome doom,
Kilmeny shall smile in eternal bloom ! "

They bore her away, she wist not how,
For she felt not arm nor rest below ;
But so swift they wained her through the light,
'Twas like the motion of sound or sight ;
They seemed to split the gales of air,
And yet nor gale nor breeze was there.
Unnumbered groves below them grew,
They came, they past, and backward flew,
Like floods of blossoms gliding on,
In moment seen, in moment gone.
O, never vales to mortal view
Appeared like those o'er which they flew !
That land to human spirits given,
The lowermost vales of the storied heaven ;
From thence they can view the world below,
And heaven's blue gates with sapphires glow,
More glory yet unmeet to know.

They bore her far to a mountain green,
To see what mortal never had seen ;
And they seated her high on a purple sward,
And bade her heed what she saw and heard,
And note the changes the spirits wrought,
For now she lived in the land of thought.
She looked, and she saw nor sun nor skies,
But a crystal dome of a thousand dies :
She looked, and she saw nae land aright,
But an endless whirl of glory and light :
And radiant beings went and came
Far swifter than wind, or the linked flame.
She hid her een frae the dazzling view ;
She looked again, and the scene was new.

She saw a sun on a summer sky,
And clouds of amber sailing bye ;
A lovely land beneath her lay,
And that land had glens and mountains gray ;
And that land had valleys and hoary piles,
And marled seas, and a thousand isles ;
Its fields were speckled, its forests green,
And its lakes were all of the dazzling sheen,
Like magic mirrors, where slumbering lay
The sun and the sky and the cloudlet gray ;
Which heaved and trembled, and gently swung,
On every shore they seemed to be hung ;
For there they were seen on their downward plain
A thousand times and a thousand again ;
In winding lake and placid firth,
Little peaceful heavens in the bosom of earth.

Kilmeny sighed and seemed to grieve,
For she found her heart to that land did cleave ;
She saw the corn wave on the vale,
She saw the deer run down the dale ;

She saw the plaid and the broad claymore,
And the brows that the badge of freedom bore ;
And she thought she had seen the land before.

She saw a lady sit on a throne,
The fairest that ever the sun shone on !
A lion licked her hand of milk,
And she held him in a leish of silk ;
And a leifu' maiden stood at her knee,
With a silver wand and melting ee ;
Her sovereign shield till love stole in,
And poisoned all the fount within.

Then a gruff untoward bedes-man came,
And hundit the lion on his dame ;
And the guardian maid wi' the dauntless ee,
She dropped a tear, and left her knee ;
And she saw till the queen frae the lion fled,
Till the bonniest flower of the world lay dead ;
A coffin was set on a distant plain,
And she saw the red blood fall like rain :
Then bonny Kilmeny's heart grew sair,
And she turned away, and could look nae mair.

Then the gruff grim carle girned amain,
And they trampled him down, but he rose again ;
And he baited the lion to deeds of weir,
Till he lapped the blood to the kingdom dear ;
And weening his head was danger-preef,
When crowned with the rose and clover leaf,
He gowled at the carle, and chased him away
To feed wi' the deer on the mountain gray.
He gowled at the carle, and he gecked at Heaven,
But his mark was set, and his arles given.
Kilmeny a while her een withdrew ;
She looked again, and the scene was new.

She saw below her fair unfurled
One half of all the glowing world,
Where oceans rolled, and rivers ran,
To bound the aims of sinful man.
She saw a people, fierce and fell,
Burst frae their bounds like fiends of hell ;
There lilies grew, and the eagle flew,
And she herked on her ravening crew,
Till the cities and towers were wrapt in a blaze,
And the thunder it roared o'er the lands and the seas.
The widows they wailed, and the red blood ran,
And she threatened an end to the race of man ;
She never lened, nor stood in awe,
Till claught by the lion's deadly paw.
Oh ! then the eagle swinked for life,
And brainzelled up a mortal strife ;
But flew she north, or flew she south,
She met wi' the gowl of the lion's mouth.

With a mooted wing and waefu' maen,
The eagle sought her eiry again ;
But lang may she cower in her bloody nest,
And lang, lang sleek her wounded breast,
Before she sey another flight,
To play wi' the norland lion's might.

But to sing the sights Kilmeny saw,
So far surpassing nature's law,
The singer's voice wad sink away,
And the string of his harp wad cease to play.
But she saw till the sorrows of man were bye,
And all was love and harmony ;
Till the stars of heaven fell calmly away,
Like the flakes of snaw on a winter day.

Then Kilmeny begged again to see
The friends she had left in her own countrye,
To tell of the place where she had been,
And the glories that lay in the land unseen ;
To warn the living maidens fair,
The loved of Heaven, the spirits' care,
That all whose minds unmeled remain
Shall bloom in beauty when time is gane.

With distant music, soft and deep,
They lulled Kilmeny sound asleep ;
And when she awakened, she lay her lane,
All happed with flowers in the green-wood wene.
When seven lang years had come and fled ;
When grief was calm, and hope was dead ;
When scarce was remembered Kilmeny's name,
Late, late in a gloamin Kilmeny came hame !
And O, her beauty was fair to see,
But still and steadfast was her ee !
Such beauty bard may never declare,
For there was no pride nor passion there ;
And the soft desire of maiden's een
In that mild face could never be seen.
Her seymar was the lily flower,
And her cheek the moss-rose in the shower ;
And her voice like the distant melodye,
That floats along the twilight sea.
But she loved to raike the lanely glen,
And keeped afar frae the haunts of men ;
Her holy hymns unheard to sing,
To suck the flowers, and drink the spring.
But wherever her peaceful form appeared,
The wild beasts of the hill were cheered ;
The wolf played blythly round the field,
The lordly byson lowed and kneeled ;
The dun deer wooed with manner bland,
And cowered aneath her lily hand.

And when at even the woodlands rung,
When hymns of other worlds she sung
In ecstasy of sweet devotion,
O, then the glen was all in motion !
The wild beasts of the forest came,
Broke from their bughts and faulds the tame,
And goved around, charmed and amazed ;
Even the dull cattle crooned and gazed,
And murmured and looked with anxious pain
For something the mystery to explain.
The buzzard came with the throstle-cock ;
The corby left her houf in the rock ;
The blackbird alang wi' the eagle flew ;
The hind came tripping o'er the dew ;
The wolf and the kid their raike began,
And the tod, and the lamb, and the leveret ran ;
The hawk and the hern attour them hung,
And the merl and the mavis forhooyed their young ;
And all in a peaceful ring were hurled :
It was like an eve in a sinless world !

When a month and a day had come and gane,
Kilmeny sought the green-wood wene ;
There laid her down on the leaves sae green,
And Kilmeny on earth was never mair seen.
But O, the words that fell from her mouth,
Were words of wonder, and words of truth !
But all the land were in fear and dread,
For they kendna whether she was living or dead.
It wasna her hame, and she couldna remain ;
She left this world of sorrow and pain,
And returned to the land of thought again.

THE MERMAID

" OH where won ye, my bonnie lass,
    Wi' look sae wild an' cheery ?
There's something in that witching face
    That I lo'e wonder dearly."

" I live where the hare-bell never grew,
    Where the streamlet never ran,
Where the winds o' heaven never blew ;
    Now find me gin you can."

" 'Tis but your wild an' wily way,
    The gloaming maks you eirie,
For ye are the lass o' the Braken-Brae,
    An' nae lad maun come near ye :

" But I am sick, an' very sick
    Wi' a passion strange an' new,
For ae kiss o' thy rosy cheek
    An' lips o' the coral hue."

" O laith, laith wad a wanderer be
    To do your youth sic wrang ;
Were you to reave a kiss from me
    Your life would not be lang.

" Go hie you from this lonely brake,
    Nor dare your walk renew ;
For I'm the Maid of the Mountain Lake,
    An' I come wi' the falling dew."

" Be you the Maid of the Crystal Wave,
    Or she of the Braken-Brae,
One tender kiss I mean to have ;
    You shall not say me nay.

B

" For beauty's like the daisy's vest
  That shrinks from the early dew,
But soon it opes its bonnie breast,
  An' sae may it fare wi' you."

" Kiss but this hand, I humbly sue,
  Even there I'll rue the stain ;
Or the breath of man will dim its hue,
  It will ne'er be pure again.

" For passion's like the burning beal
  Upon the mountain's brow,
That wastes itself to ashes pale ;
  An' sae will it fare wi' you."

———

" O mother, mother, make my bed,
  An' make it soft and easy ;
An' with the cold dew bathe my head,
  For pains of anguish seize me :

" Or stretch me in the chill blue lake,
  To quench this bosom's burning ;
An' lay me by yon lonely brake,
  For hope there's none returning.

" I've been where man should not have been,
  Oft in my lonely roaming ;
And seen what man should not have seen,
  By greenwood in the gloaming.

" Oh, passion's deadlier than the grave,
  A' human things undoing !
The Maiden of the Mountain Wave
  Has lured me to my ruin ! "

———

'Tis now an hundred years an' more,
   An' all these scenes are over,
Since rose his grave on yonder shore,
   Beneath the wild wood cover ;

An' late I saw the Maiden there,
   Just as the day-light faded,
Braiding her locks of gowden hair,
   An' singing as she braided :

MERMAID'S SONG

Lie still, my love, lie still and sleep,
   Long is thy night of sorrow ;
Thy Maiden of the Mountain deep
   Shall meet thee on the morrow.

But oh, when shall that morrow be,
   That my true love shall waken ?
When shall we meet, refined an' free,
   Amid the moorland braken ?

Full low and lonely is thy bed,
   The worm even flies thy pillow ;
Where now the lips, so comely red,
   That kissed me 'neath the willow ?

Oh I must laugh, do as I can,
   Even 'mid my song of mourning,
At all the fuming freaks of man
   To which there's no returning.

Lie still, my love, lie still an' sleep—
   Hope lingers o'er thy slumber ;
What though thy years beneath the steep
   Should all its stones outnumber ?

Though moons steal o'er an' seasons fly
  On time's swift wing unstaying,
Yet there's a spirit in the sky
  That lives o'er thy decaying.

In domes beneath the water-springs
  No end hath my sojourning ;
An' to this land of fading things
  Far hence be my returning ;

For spirits now have left the deep,
  Their long last farewell taken :
Lie still, my love, lie still an' sleep,
  Thy day is near the breaking !

When my loved flood from fading day
  No more its gleam shall borrow,
Nor heath-fowl from the moorland gray,
  Bid the blue dawn good-morrow ;

The Mermaid o'er thy grave shall weep,
  Without one breath of scorning :
Lie still, my love, lie still an' sleep,
  And fare thee well till morning !

A WITCH'S CHANT

THOU art weary, weary, weary,
Thou art weary and far away !
Hear me, gentle spirit, hear me ;
Come before the dawn of day.

I hear a small voice from the hill,
 The vapour is deadly, pale, and still—
A murmuring sough is on the wood,
And the witching star is red as blood.

And in the cleft of heaven I scan
The giant form of a naked man ;
His eye is like the burning brand,
And he holds a sword in his right hand.

All is not well : by dint of spell,
Somewhere between the heaven and hell
There is this night a wild deray ;
The spirits have wander'd from their way.

The purple drops shall tinge the moon,
As she wanders through the midnight noon ;
And the dawning heaven shall all be red
With blood by guilty angels shed.

Be as it will, I have the skill
To work by good or work by ill ;
Then here's for pain, and here's for thrall,
And here's for conscience, worst of all !

Another chant, and then, and then,
Spirits shall come or Christian men—
Come from the earth, the air, or the sea :
Great Gil-Moules, I cry to thee !

Sleep'st thou, wakest thou, lord of the wind !
Mount thy steeds and gallop them blind ;
And the long-tailed fiery dragon outfly,
The rocket of heaven, the bomb of the sky.

Over the dog-star, over the wain,
Over the cloud, and the rainbow's mane,
Over the mountain, and over the sea,
Haste—haste—haste to me !

Then here's for trouble and here's for smart,
And here's for the pang that seeks the heart ;
Here's for madness, and here's for thrall,
And here's for conscience, the worst of all !

THE WITCH OF FIFE

" Quhare haif ye been, ye ill womyne,
   These three lang nightis fra hame ?
Quhat garris the sweit drap fra yer brow,
   Like clotis of the saut sea faem ?

" It fearis me muckil ye haif seen
   Quhat guid man never knew ;
It fearis me muckil ye haif been
   Quhare the gray cock never crew.

" But the spell may crack, and the brydel breck,
   Then sherpe yer werde will be ;
Ye had better sleipe in yer bed at hame,
   Wi' yer deire littil bairnis and me."—

" Sit doune, sit doune, my leil auld man,
   Sit doune, and listin to me ;
I'll gar the hayre stand on yer crown,
   And the cauld sweit blind yer ee.

" But tell nae wordis, my guid auld man,
   Tell never word again ;
Or deire shall be yer courtisye,
   And driche and sair yer pain.

" The first leet night, quhan the new moon set,
   Quhan all was douffe and mirk,
We saddled ouir naigis wi' the moon-fern leif,
   And rode fra Kilmerrin kirk.

" Some horses ware of the brume-cow framit,
   And some of the greine bay tree ;
But mine was made of ane humloke schaw,
   And a stout stallion was he.

" We raide the tod doune on the hill,
  The martin on the law ;
And we huntyd the hoolet out of brethe,
  And forcit him doune to fa."—

" Quhat guid was that, ye ill womyne ?
  Quhat guid was that to thee ?
Ye wald better haif been in yer bed at hame,
  Wi' yer deire littil bairnis and me."—

" And aye we raide, and se merrily we raide,
  Throw the merkist gloffis of the night ;
And we swam the floode, and we darnit the woode,
  Till we cam to the Lommond height.

" And quhan we cam to the Lommond height,
  Se lythlye we lychtid doune ;
And we drank fra the hornis that never grew,
  The beer that was never browin.

" Then up there raise ane wee wee man,
  Fra nethe the moss-gray stane ;
His fece was wan like the collifloure,
  For he nouthir had blude nor bane.

" He set ane reid-pipe til his muthe,
  And he playit se bonnilye,
Till the gray curlew and the black-cock flew
  To listen his melodye.

" It rang se sweit through the grein Lommond,
  That the nycht-winde lowner blew ;
And it soupit alang the Loch Leven,
  And wakinit the white sea-mew.

" It rang se sweit through the grein Lommond,
  Se sweitly butt and se shill,
That the wezilis laup out of their mouldy holis,
  And dancit on the mydnycht hill.

" The corby craw cam gledgin near,
    The ern gede veeryng bye ;
And the troutis laup out of the Leven Loch,
    Charmit with the melodye.

" And aye we dancit on the grein Lommond,
    Till the dawn on the ocean grew :
Ne wonder I was a weary wycht
    Quhan I cam hame to you."—

" Quhat guid, quhat guid, my weird weird wyfe,
    Quhat guid was that to thee ?
Ye wald better haif bein in yer bed at hame,
    Wi' her deire littil bairnis and me."

" The second nycht, quhan the new moon set,
    O'er the roaryng sea we flew ;
The cockle-shell our trusty bark,
    Our sailis of the grein sea-rue.

" And the bauld windis blew, and the fire-flauchtis
        flew,
    And the sea ran to the skie ;
And the thunner it growlit, and the sea-dogs howlit,
    As we gaed scouryng bye.

" And aye we mountit the sea-grein hillis,
    Quhill we brushit thro' the cludis of the hevin ;
Than sousit dounright like the stern-shot light,
    Fra the liftis blue casement driven.

" But our taickil stood, and our bark was good,
    And se pang was our pearily prowe ;
Quhan we culdna speil the brow of the wavis,
    We needilit them throu belowe.

" As fast as the hail, as fast as the gale,
    As fast as the mydnycht leme,
  We borit the breiste of the burstyng swale,
    Or fluffit i' the flotyng faem.

" And quhan to the Norraway shore we wan,
    We muntyd our steedis of the wynde,
  And we splashit the floode, and we darnit the woode,
    And we left the shouir behynde.

" Fleit is the roe on the grein Lommond,
    And swift is the couryng grew ;
  The rein-deir dun can eithly run,
    Quhan the houndis and the hornis pursue.

" But nowther the roe, nor the rein-deir dun,
    The hinde nor the couryng grew,
  Culde fly owr muntaine, muir, and dale,
    As our braw steedis they flew.

" The dales war deep, and the Doffrinis steep,
    And we raise to the skyis ee-bree ;
  Quhite, quhite was our rode, that was never trode,
    Owr the snawis of eternity !

" And quhan we cam to the Lapland lone,
    The fairies war all in array ;
  For all the genii of the north
    War keipyng their holeday.

" The warlock men and the weird wemyng,
    And the fays of the wood and the steip,
  And the phantom hunteris all war there,
    And the mermaidis of the deip.

" And they washit us all with the witch-water,
    Distillit fra the muirland dew,
Quhill our beauty blumit like the Lapland rose,
    That wylde in the foreste grew."—

" Ye lee, ye lee, ye ill womyne,
    Se loud as I heir ye lee !
For the warst-faurd wyfe on the shoris of Fyfe
    Is cumlye comparit wi' thee."—

" Then the mermaidis sang and the woodlandis rang,
    Se sweitly swellit the quire ;
On every cliff a herpe they hang,
    On every tree a lyre.

" And aye they sang, and the woodlandis rang,
    And we drank, and we drank se deip ;
Then soft in the armis of the warlock men,
    We laid us dune to sleip."—

" Away, away, ye ill womyne,
    An ill deide met ye dee !
Quhan ye hae pruvit se false to yer God,
    Ye can never pruve true to me."—

" And there we learnit fra the fairy foke,
    And fra our master true,
The wordis that can beire us throu the air,
    And lokkis and barris undo.

" Last nycht we met at Maisry's cot ;
    Richt weil the wordis we knew ;
And we set a foot on the black cruik-shell,
    And out at the lum we flew.

" And we flew owr hill, and we flew owr dale,
    And we flew owr firth and sea,
Until we cam to merry Carlisle,
    Quhare we lightit on the lea.

" We gaed to the vault beyound the towir,
    Quhare we enterit free as ayr ;
And we drank, and we drank of the bishopis wine
    Quhill we culde drynk ne mair."—

" Gin that be true, my guid auld wyfe,
    Whilk thou hast tauld to me,
Betide my death, betide my lyfe,
    I'll beire thee companye.

" Neist tyme ye gaung to merry Carlisle
    To drynk of the blude-reid wyne,
Beshrew my heart, I'll fly with thee,
    If the deil should fly behynde."

" Ah ! little do ye ken, my silly auld man,
    The daingeris we maun dree ;
Last nychte we drank of the bishopis wyne,
    Quhill near near taen war we.

" Afore we wan to the Sandy Ford,
    The gor-cockis nichering flew ;
The lofty crest of Ettrick Pen
    Was wavit about with blue,
And, flichtering throu the ayr, we fand
    The chill chill mornyng dew.

" As we flew owr the hillis of Braid,
    The sun raise fair and cleir ;
Their gurly James, and his baronis braw,
    War out to hunt the deir.

" Their bowis they drew, their arrowis flew,
　　And piercit the ayr with speide,
Quhill purpil fell the mornyng dew
　　With witch-blude rank and reide.

" Littil do ye ken, my silly auld man,
　　The daingeris we maun dree ;
Ne wonder I am a weary wycht
　　Quhan I come hame to thee."—

" But tell me the *word*, my guid auld wyfe,
　　Come tell it me speedilye :
For I lang to drynk of the guid reide wyne,
　　And to wyng the ayr with thee.

" Yer hellish horse I wilna ryde,
　　Nor sail the seas in the wynde ;
But I can flee as weil as thee,
　　And I'll drynk quhill ye be blynd."—

" O fy ! O fy ! my leil auld man,
　　That word I darena tell ;
It wald turn this warld all upside down,
　　And make it warse than hell.

" For all the lasses in the land
　　Wald munt the wynde and fly ;
And the men wald doff their doublets syde,
　　And after them wald ply."—

But the auld guidman was ane cunnyng auld man,
　　And ane cunnyng auld man was he ;
And he watchit, and he watchit for mony a nychte,
　　The witches' flychte to see.

Ane nychte he darnit in Maisry's cot ;
   The fearless haggs cam in ;
And he heard the word of awsome weird,
   And he saw their deidis of synn.

Then ane by ane they said that word,
   As fast to the fire they drew ;
Then set a foot on the black cruik-shell,
   And out at the lum they flew.

The auld guidman cam fra his hole
   With feire and muckil dreide,
But yet he culdna think to rue,
   For the wyne cam in his head.

He set his foot in the black cruik-shell,
   With ane fixit and ane wawlyng ee ;
And he said the word that I darena say,
   And out at the lum flew he.

The witches skalit the moon-beam pale ;
   Deep groanit the trembling wynde ;
But they never wist till our auld guidman
   Was hoveryng them behynde.

They flew to the vaultis of merry Carlisle,
   Quhare they enterit free as ayr ;
And they drank and they drank of the bishopis
     wyne
   Quhill they culde drynk ne mair.

The auld guidman he grew se crouse,
   He dancit on the mouldy ground,
And he sang the bonniest sangs of Fyfe,
   And he tuzzlit the kerlyngs round.

And aye he piercit the tither butt,
    And he suckit, and he suckit se lang,
Quhill his een they closit, and his voice grew low,
    And his tongue wald hardly gang.

The kerlyngs drank of the bishopis wyne
    Quhill they scentit the morning wynde ;
Then clove again the yielding ayr,
    And left the auld man behynde.

And aye he sleipit on the damp damp floor,
    He sleipit and he snorit amain ;
He never dreamit he was far fra hame,
    Or that the auld wyvis war gane.

And aye he sleipit on the damp damp floor,
    Quhill past the mid-day highte,
Quhan wakenit by five rough Englishmen,
    That trailit him to the lychte.

" Now quha are ye, ye silly auld man,
    That sleipis se sound and se weil ?
  Or how gat ye into the bishopis vault
    Through lokkis and barris of steel ? "

The auld gudeman he tryit to speak,
    But ane word he culdna fynde ;
He tryit to think, but his head whirlit round,
    And ane thing he culdna mynde :—
" I am fra Fyfe," the auld man cryit,
    " And I cam on the mydnycht wynde."

They nickit the auld man, and they prickit the
    man
    And they yerkit his limbis with twine,
Quhill the reide blude ran in his hose and shoon,
    But some cryit it was wyne.

They lickit the auld man, and they prickit the
    auld man,
  And they tyit him till ane stone ;
And they set ane bele-fire him about,
  To burn him skin and bone.

" O wae to me ! " said the puir auld man,
  " That ever I saw the day !
And wae be to all the ill wemyng
  That lead puir men astray !

" Let nevir ane auld man after this
    To lawless greide inclyne ;
  Let nevir ane auld man after this
    Rin post to the deil for wyne."

The reike flew up in the auld manis face,
  And choukit him bitterlye ;
And the lowe cam up with ane angry blese,
  And it syngit his auld breek-knee.

He lukit to the land fra whence he cam,
  For lukis he culde get ne mae ;
And he thochte of his deire littil bairnis at hame,
  And O the auld man was wae !

But they turnit their facis to the sun,
  With gloffe and wonderous glair,
For they saw ane thing beth lairge and dun,
  Comin swaipin down the ayr.

That burd it cam fra the landis o' Fyfe,
  And it cam rycht tymeouslye,
For quha was it but the auld manis wife,
  Just comit his dethe to see.

Scho put ane reide cap on his heide,
    And the auld guidman lookit fain,
Then whisperit ane word intil his lug,
    And tovit to the ayr again.

The auld guidman he gae ane bob
    I' the mids o' the burnyng lowe :
And the sheklis that band him to the ring,
    They fell fra his armis like towe.

He drew his breath, and he said the word,
    And he said it with muckil glee,
Then set his fit on the burnyng pile,
    And away to the ayr flew he.

Till aince he cleirit the swirlyng reike,
    He lukit beth ferit and sad ;
But whan he wan to the lycht blue ayr,
    He lauchit as he'd been mad.

His armis war spred, and his heid was hiche,
    And his feite stack out behynde ;
And the laibies of the auld manis cote
    War wauffing in the wynde.

And aye he neicherit, and aye he flew,
    For he thochte the ploy se raire ;
It was like the voice of the gainder blue,
    Quhan he flees throu the ayr.

He lukit back to the Carlisle men
    As he borit the norlan sky ;
He noddit his heide, and gae ane girn,
    But he nevir said guid-bye.

They vanisht far i' the liftis blue wale,
  Ne mair the English saw,
But the auld manis lauche cam on the gale,
  With a lang and a loud gaffa.

May everilke man in the land of Fyfe
  Read what the drinkeris dree ;
And nevir curse his puir auld wife,
  Rychte wicked altho scho be.

THE FLYING TAILOR

Being A Further Extract from The Recluse, a Poem

If ever chance or choice thy footsteps lead
Into that green and flowery burial-ground
That compasseth with sweet and mournful smiles
The church of Grassmere,—by the eastern gate
Enter—and underneath a stunted yew,
Some three yards distant from the gravel-walk,
On the left-hand side, thou wilt espy a grave,
With unelaborate head-stone beautified,
Conspicuous 'mid the other stoneless heaps
'Neath which the children of the valley lie.
There pause—and with no common feelings read
This short inscription—" Here lies buried
The Flying Tailor, aged twenty-nine ! "

Him from his birth unto his death I knew,
And many years before he had attained
The fulness of his fame, I prophesied
The triumphs of that youth's agility,
And crowned him with that name which afterwards
He nobly justified—and dying left
To fame's eternal blazon—read it here—
" The Flying Tailor ! "

C

It is somewhat strange
That his mother was a cripple, and his father
Long way declined into the vale of years,
When their son Hugh was born.   At first the babe
Was sickly, and a smile was seen to pass
Across the midwife's cheek, when, holding up
The sickly wretch, she to the father said,
" A fine man-child ! "   What else could they expect ?
The mother being, as I said before,
A cripple, and the father of the child
Long way declined into the vale of years.

But mark the wondrous change—ere he was put
By his mother into breeches, Nature strung
The muscular part of his economy
To an unusual strength, and he could leap,
All unimpeded by his petticoats,
Over the stool on which his mother sat
When carding wool, or cleansing vegetables,
Or meek performing other household tasks.
Cunning he watched his opportunity,
And oft, as house affairs did call her thence,
Overleapt Hugh, a perfect whirligig,
More than six inches o'er the astonished stool !

What boots it to narrate, how at leap-frog
Over the breeched and unbreeched villagers
He shone conspicuous ?   Leap-frog do I say ?
Vainly so named.   What though in attitude
The Flying Tailor aped the croaking race
When issuing from the weed-entangled pool,
Tadpoles no more, they seek the new-mown fields,
A jocund people, bouncing to and fro
Amid the odorous clover—while amazed
The grasshopper sits idle on the stalk
With folded pinions and forgets to sing.

Frog-like, no doubt, in attitude he was ;
But sure his bounds across the village green
Seemed to my soul—(my soul for ever bright
With purest beams of sacred poesy)—
Like bounds of red-deer on the Highland hill,
When, close environed by the tinchel's chain,
He lifts his branchy forehead to the sky,
Then o'er the many-headed multitude
Springs belling half in terror, half in rage,
And fleeter than the sun-beam or the wind
Speeds to his cloud-lair on the mountain-top.

No more of this—suffice it to narrate,
In his tenth year he was apprenticed
Unto a Master Tailor, by a strong
And regular indenture of seven years,
Commencing from the date the parchment bore,
And ending on a certain day, that made
The term complete of seven solar years.
Oft have I heard him say, that at this time
Of life he was most wretched ; for, constrained
To sit all day cross-legged upon a board,
The natural circulation of the blood
Thereby was oft impeded, and he felt
So numbed at times, that when he strove to rise
Up from his work, he could not, but fell back
Among the shreds and patches that bestrewed
With various colours, brightening gorgeously,
The board all round him—patch of warlike red
With which he patched the regimental suits
Of a recruiting military troop,
At that time stationed in a market-town
At no great distance—eke of solemn black
Shreds of no little magnitude, with which
The parson's Sunday-coat was then repairing,
That in the new-roofed church he might appear
With fitting dignity—and gravely fill

The sacred seat of pulpit eloquence,
Cheering with doctrinal point and words of faith
The poor man's heart, and from the shallow wit
Of atheist drying up each argument,
Or sharpening his own weapons, only to turn
Their point against himself, and overthrow
His idols with the very enginery
Reared 'gainst the structure of our English church.

Oft too, when striving all he could to finish
The stated daily task, the needle's point,
Slanting insidious from the eluded stitch,
Hath pinched his finger, by the thimble's mail
In vain defended, and the crimson blood
Distained the lining of some wedding-suit ;
A dismal omen ! that to mind like his,
Apt to perceive in slightest circumstance
Mysterious meaning, yielded sore distress
And feverish perturbation, so that oft
He scarce could eat his dinner—nay, one night
He swore to run from his apprenticeship,
And go on board a first-rate man-of-war,
From Plymouth lately come to Liverpool,
Where, in the stir and tumult of a crew
Composed of many nations, 'mid the roar
Of wave and tempest, and the deadlier voice
Of battle, he might strive to mitigate
The fever that consumed his mighty heart.

But other doom was his.   That very night
A troop of tumblers came into the village,
Tumbler, equestrian, mountebank—on wire,
On rope, on horse, with cup and balls, intent
To please the gaping multitude, and win
The coin from labour's pocket—small perhaps
Each separate piece of money, but when joined
Making a good round sum, destined ere long

All to be melted, (so these lawless folk
Name spending coin in loose debauchery),
Melted into ale—or haply stouter cheer,
Gin diuretic, or the liquid flame
Of baneful brandy, by the smuggler brought
From the French coast in shallop many-oared,
Skulking by night round headland and through bay,
Afraid of the king's cutter, or the barge
Of cruising frigate, armed with chosen men,
And with her sweeps across the foamy waves
Moving most beautiful with measured strokes.

   It chanced that as he threw a somerset
Over three horses (each of larger size
Than our small mountain-breed), one of the troop
Put out his shoulder, and was otherwise
Considerably bruised, especially
About the loins and back.   So he became
Useless unto that wandering company,
And likely to be felt a sore expense
To men just on the eve of bankruptcy ;
So the master of the troop determined
To leave him in the work-house, and proclaimed
That if there was a man among the crowd
Willing to fill his place and able too,
Now was the time to shew himself.   Hugh Thwaites
Heard the proposal, as he stood apart
Striving with his own soul—and with a bound
He leapt into the circle, and agreed
To supply the place of him who had been hurt.
A shout of admiration and surprise
Then tore heaven's concave, and completely filled
The little field, where near a hundred people
Were standing in a circle round and fair.
Oft have I striven by meditative power,
And reason working 'mid the various forms
Of various occupations and professions,

To explain the cause of one phenomenon,
That, since the birth of science, hath remained
A bare enunciation, unexplained
By any theory, or mental light
Streamed on it by the imaginative will,
Or spirit musing in the cloudy shrine,
The penetralia of the immortal soul.
I now allude to that most curious fact,
That 'mid a given number, say threescore,
Of tailors, more men of agility
Will issue out, than from an equal shew
From any other occupation—say
Smiths, barbers, bakers, butchers, or the like.
Let me not seem presumptuous, if I strive
This subject to illustrate ; nor, while I give
My meditations to the world, will I
Conceal from it, that much I have to say
I learnt from one who knows the subject well
In theory and practice—need I name him ?
The light-heeled author of the Isle of Palms,
Illustrious more for leaping than for song.

First, then, I would lay down this principle,
That all excessive action by the law
Of nature tends unto repose.   This granted,
All action not excessive must partake
The nature of excessive action—so
That in all human beings who keep moving,
Unconscious cultivation of repose
Is going on in silence.   Be it so.
Apply to men of sedentary lives
This leading principle, and we behold
That, active in their inactivity,
And unreposing in their long repose,
They are, in fact, the sole depositaries
Of all the energies by others wasted,
And come at last to teem with impulses

Of muscular motion, not to be withstood,
And either giving vent unto themselves
In numerous feats of wild agility,
Or terminating in despair and death.

Now, of all sedentary lives, none seems
So much so as the tailor's.—Weavers use
Both arms and legs, and, we may safely add,
Their bodies too, for arms and legs can't move
Without the body—as the waving branch
Of the green oak disturbs his glossy trunk.
Not so the tailor—for he sits cross-legged,
Cross-legged for ever ! save at time of meals,
In bed, or when he takes his little walk
From shop to alehouse, picking, as he goes,
Stray patch of fustian, cloth, or cassimere,
Which, as by natural instinct, he discerns,
Though soiled with mud, and by the passing wheel
Bruised to attenuation 'gainst the stones.

Here then we pause—and need no farther go ;
We have reached the sea-mark of our utmost sail.
Now let me trace the effect upon his mind
Of this despised profession.   Deem not thou,
O rashly deem not, that his boyish days
Past at the shop-board, when the stripling bore
With bashful feeling of apprenticeship
The name of Tailor ; deem not that his soul
Derived no genial influence from a life,
Which, although haply adverse in the main
To the growth of intellect, and the excursive power,
Yet in its ordinary forms possessed
A constant influence o'er his passing thoughts,
Moulded his appetences and his will,
And wrought out, by the work of sympathy
Between his bodily and mental form,
Rare correspondence, wondrous unity !

Perfect—complete—and fading not away.
While on his board cross-legged he used to sit,
Shaping of various garments, to his mind
An image rose of every character
For whom each special article was framed,
Coat, waistcoat, breeches.   So at last his soul
Was like a storehouse, filled with images,
By musing hours of solitude supplied.
Nor did his ready fingers shape the cut
Of villager's uncouth habiliments
With greater readiness, than did his mind
Frame corresponding images of those
Whose corporal measurement the neat-marked paper
In many a mystic notch for aye retained.
Hence, more than any man I ever knew,
Did he possess the power intuitive
Of diving into character.   A pair
Of breeches, to his philosophic eye,
Were not what unto other folks they seem,
Mere simple breeches, but in them he saw
The symbol of the soul—mysterious, high
Hieroglyphics ! such as Egypt's Priest
Adored upon the holy Pyramid,
Vainly imagined tomb of monarchs old,
But raised by wise philosophy, that sought
By darkness to illumine, and to spread
Knowledge by dim concealment—process high
Of man's imaginative, deathless soul.
Nor, haply, in the abasement of the life
Which stern necessity had made his own,
Did he not recognise a genial power
Of soul-ennobling fortitude.   He heard
Unmoved the witling's shallow contumely,
And thus, in spite of nature, by degrees
He saw a beauty and a majesty
In this despised trade, which warrior's brow
Hath rarely circled—so that when he sat

Beneath his sky-light window, he hath cast
A gaze of triumph on the godlike sun,
And felt that orb, in all his annual round,
Beheld no happier, nobler character
Than him, Hugh Thwaites, a little tailor boy.

Thus I, with no unprofitable song,
Have, in the silence of the umbrageous wood,
Chaunted the heroic youthful attributes
Of him the Flying Tailor.   Much remains
Of highest argument, to lute or lyre
Fit to be murmured with impassioned voice ;
And when, by timely supper and by sleep
Refreshed, I turn me to the welcome task,
With lofty hopes—Reader, do thou expect
The final termination of my lay.
For, mark my words,—eternally my name
Shall last on earth, conspicuous like a star
'Mid that bright galaxy of favoured spirits,
Who, laughed at constantly whene'er they published,
Survived the impotent scorn of base Reviews,
Monthly or Quarterly, or that accursed
Journal, the Edinburgh Review, that lives
On tears, and sighs, and groans, and brains, and blood.

WALSINGHAME'S SONG

(From " Wat o' the Cleuch ")

O HEARD ye never of Wat o' the Cleuch ?
The lad that has worrying tikes enow,
Whose meat is the moss, and whose drink is the dew,
And that's the cheer of Wat o' the Cleuch.
        Wat o' the Cleuch ! Wat o' the Cleuch !
        Woe's my heart for Wat o' the Cleuch !

Wat o' the Cleuch sat down to dine
With two pint stoups of good red wine ;
But when he looked they both were dry ;
Oh, poverty parts good company !
    Wat o' the Cleuch ! Wat o' the Cleuch !
    O for a drink to Wat o' the Cleuch !

Wat o' the Cleuch came down the Tyne,
To woo a maid both gallant and fine ;
But as he came o'er by Dick o' the Side,
He smelled the mutton and left the bride.
    Wat o' the Cleuch ! Wat o' the Cleuch !
    What think ye now of Wat o' the Cleuch ?

Wat o' the Cleuch came here to steal,
He wanted milk, and he wanted veal :
But ere he wan o'er the Beetleston brow
He houghed the calf and eated the cow !
    Wat o' the Cleuch ! Wat o' the Cleuch !
    Well done, doughty Wat o' the Cleuch !

Wat o' the Cleuch came here to fight,
But his whittle was blunt, and his nag took fright,
And the braggart he did what I dare not tell,
But changed his cheer at the back of the fell.
    Wat o' the Cleuch ! Wat o' the Cleuch !
    O for a croudy to Wat o' the Cleuch !

Wat o' the Cleuch kneeled down to pray,
He wist not what to do or say ;
But he prayed for beef, and he prayed for bree,
A two-handed spoon and a haggies to pree.
    Wat o' the Cleuch ! Wat o' the Cleuch !
    That's the cheer for Wat o' the Cleuch !

But the devil is cunning as I heard say,
He knew his right, and hauled him away !
And he's over the Border and over the heuch,
And off to hell with Wat o' the Cleuch.
>   Wat o' the Cleuch !   Wat o' the Cleuch !
>   Lack-a-day for Wat o' the Cleuch !

But of all the wights in poor Scotland,
That ever drew bow or Border brand,
That ever drove English bullock or ewe,
There never was thief like Wat o' the Cleuch.
>   Wat o' the Cleuch !   Wat o' the Cleuch !
>   Down for ever with Wat o' the Cleuch !

LOCK THE DOOR, LARISTON

Lock the door, Lariston, lion of Liddisdale,
Lock the door, Lariston, Lowther comes on,
>   The Armstrongs are flying,
>   Their widows are crying,
The Castletown's burning, and Oliver's gone ;
Lock the door, Lariston—high on the weather gleam
See how the Saxon plumes bob on the sky,
>   Yeoman and carbineer,
>   Billman and halberdier ;
Fierce is the foray, and far is the cry.

Bewcastle brandishes high his broad scimitar,
Ridley is riding his fleet-footed grey,
>   Hedley and Howard there,
>   Wandale and Windermere,—
Lock the door, Lariston, hold them at bay.
Why dost thou smile, noble Elliot of Lariston ?
Why do the joy-candles gleam in thine eye ?
>   Thou bold Border ranger,
>   Beware of thy danger—
Thy foes are relentless, determined, and nigh.

Jock Elliot raised up his steel bonnet and lookit,
His hand grasp'd the sword with a nervous embrace ;
   " Ah, welcome, brave foemen,
    On earth there are no men
More gallant to meet in the foray or chase !
Little know you of the hearts I have hidden here,
Little know you of our moss-troopers' might,
    Lindhope and Sorby true,
    Sundhope and Milburn too,
Gentle in manner, but lions in fight !

I've Mangerton, Gornberry, Raeburn, and Netherby,
Old Sim of Whitram, and all his array ;
    Come all Northumberland,
    Teesdale and Cumberland,
Here at the Breaken Tower end shall the fray."
Scowl'd the broad sun o'er the links of green Liddisdale,
Red as the beacon-light tipp'd he the wold ;
    Many a bold martial eye
    Mirror'd that morning sky,
Never more oped on his orbit of gold !

Shrill was the bugle's note, dreadful the warrior shout,
Lances and halberds in splinters were borne ;
    Halberd and hauberk then
    Braved the claymore in vain,
Buckler and armlet in shivers were shorn.
See how they wane, the proud files of the Windermere,
Howard—Ah ! woe to thy hopes of the day !
    Hear the wide welkin rend,
    While the Scots' shouts ascend,
" Elliot of Lariston, Elliot for aye ! "

BONNIE PRINCE CHARLIE

Cam ye by Athol, lad wi' the philabeg,
Down by the Tummel, or banks o' the Garry ;
Saw ye our lads, wi' their bonnets and white cockades,
Leaving their mountains to follow Prince Charlie ?
    Follow thee ! follow thee ! wha wadna follow thee ?
    Lang hast thou loved and trusted us fairly :
    Charlie, Charlie, wha wadna follow thee,
    King o' the Highland hearts, bonny Prince Charlie ?

I hae but ae son, my gallant young Donald ;
But if I had ten, they should follow Glengary.
Health to M'Donnel, and gallant Clan-Ronald,
For these are the men that will die for their Charlie !
    Follow thee ! follow thee ! etc.

I'll to Lochiel and Appin, and kneel to them,
Down by Lord Murray, and Roy of Kildarlie ;
Brave M'Intosh he shall fly to the field with them ;
These are the lads I can trust wi' my Charlie !
    Follow thee ! follow thee ! etc.

Down through the Lowlands, down wi' the Whigamore !
Loyal true Highlanders, down wi' them rarely !
Ronald and Donald, drive on wi' the broad claymore,
Over the necks of the foes of Prince Charlie !
    Follow thee ! follow thee ! wha wadna follow thee ?
    Lang has thou loved and trusted us fairly :
    Charlie, Charlie, wha wadna follow thee,
    King o' the Highland hearts, bonny Prince Charlie ?

CHARLIE IS MY DARLING

'Twas on a Monday morning,
Right early in the year,
That Charlie came to our town,
The Young Chevalier.
    An' Charlie is my darling,
    My darling, my darling,
    Charlie is my darling,
    The Young Chevalier.

As Charlie he came up the gate,
His face shone like the day ;
I grat to see the lad come back
That had been lang away.
    An' Charlie is my darling, etc.

Then ilka bonny lassie sang,
As to the door she ran,
Our king shall hae his ain again,
An' Charlie is the man :
    For Charlie he's my darling, etc.

Outower yon moory mountain,
An' down the craigy glen,
Of naething else our lasses sing
But Charlie an' his men.
    An' Charlie he's my darling, etc.

Our Highland hearts are true an' leal,
An' glow without a stain ;
Our Highland swords are metal keen,
An' Charlie he's our ain.
    An' Charlie he's my darling,
    My darling, my darling ;
    Charlie he's my darling,
    The Young Chevalier.

McLEAN'S WELCOME

Come o'er the stream, Charlie,
Dear Charlie, brave Charlie ;
Come o'er the stream, Charlie,
And dine with McLean ;
And though you be weary,
We'll make your heart cheery,
And welcome our Charlie,
And his loyal train.
We'll bring down the track deer,
We'll bring down the black steer,
The lamb from the braken,
And doe from the glen,
The salt sea we'll harry,
And bring to our Charlie
The cream from the bothy
And curd from the pen.

Come o'er the stream, Charlie,
Dear Charlie, brave Charlie ;
Come o'er the sea, Charlie,
And dine with McLean ;
And you shall drink freely
The dews of Glen-sheerly,
That stream in the starlight
When kings do not ken,
And deep be your meed
Of the wine that is red,
To drink to your sire,
And his friend the McLean.

Come o'er the stream, Charlie,
Dear Charlie, brave Charlie ;
Come o'er the stream, Charlie,
And dine with McLean ;

If aught will invite you,
Or more will delight you,
'Tis ready, a troop of our bold Highlandmen,
All ranged on the heather,
With bonnet and feather,
Strong arms and broad claymores,
Three hundred and ten !

DONALD M'GILLAVRY

DONALD's gane up the hill hard an' hungry,
Donald's come down the hill wild an' angry ;
Donald will clear the gouk's nest cleverly ;
Here's to the king an' Donald M'Gillavry !
Come like a weigh-bauk, Donald M'Gillavry,
Come like a weigh-bauk, Donald M'Gillavry ;
Balance them fair, an' balance them cleverly,
Off wi' the counterfeit, Donald M'Gillavry !

Donald's come o'er the hill trailin' his tether, man,
As he war wud, or stang'd wi' an ether, man ;
When he gaes back, there's some will look merrily ;
Here's to King James an' Donald M'Gillavry !
Come like a weaver, Donald M'Gillavry,
Come like a weaver, Donald M'Gillavry ;
Pack on your back an elwand o' steelary,
Gie them full measure, my Donald M'Gillavry !

Donald has foughten wi' reif and roguery,
Donald has dinner'd wi' banes an' beggary ;
Better it war for whigs and whiggery
Meeting the deevil than Donald M'Gillavry.
Come like a tailor, Donald M'Gillavry,
Come like a tailor, Donald M'Gillavry ;
Push about, in an' out, thimble them cleverly—
Here's to King James an' Donald M'Gillavry !

Donald's the callant that bruiks nae tangleness,
Whigging an' prigging an' a' newfangleness ;
They maun be gane, he winna be baukit, man ;
He maun hae justice, or rarely he'll tak it, man.
Come like a cobler, Donald M'Gillavry,
Come like a cobler, Donald M'Gillavry ;
Bore them, an' yerk them, an' lingel them cleverly—
Up wi' King James an' Donald M'Gillavry !

Donald was mumpit wi' mirds and mockery,
Donald was blindit wi' bladds o' preperty ;
Arles ran high, but makings war naething, man ;
Gudeness, how Donald is flyting an' fretting, man !
Come like the deevil, Donald M'Gillavry,
Come like the deevil, Donald M'Gillavry ;
Skelp them an' scadd them pruved sae unbritherly—
Up wi' King James an' Donald M'Gillavry !

THE VILLAGE OF BALMAQUHAPPLE

D'YE ken the big village of Balmaquhapple,
The great muckle village of Balmaquhapple ?
'Tis steep'd in iniquity up to the thrapple,
An' what's to become o' poor Balmaquhapple ?
Fling a' aff your bannets, an' kneel for your life, fo'ks,
And pray to St Andrew, the god o' the Fife fo'ks ;
Gar a' the hills yout wi' sheer vociferation,
And thus you may cry on sic needfu' occasion :

" O, blessed St Andrew, if e'er ye could pity fo'k,
Men fo'k or women fo'k, country or city fo'k,
Come for this aince wi' the auld thief to grapple,
An' save the great village of Balmaquhapple

D

Frae drinking an' leeing, an' flyting an' swearing,
An' sins that ye wad be affrontit at hearing,
An' cheating an' stealing ; O, grant them redemption,
All save an' except the few after to mention :

" There's Johnny the elder, wha hopes ne'er to need ye,
Sae pawkie, sae holy, sae gruff, an' sae greedy ;
Wha prays every hour as the wayfarer passes,
But aye at a hole where he watches the lasses ;
He's cheated a thousand, an' e'en to this day yet,
Can cheat a young lass, or they're leears that say it
Then gie him his gate ; he's sae slee an' sae civil,
Perhaps in the end he may wheedle the devil.

" There's Cappie the cobbler, an' Tammie the tinman,
An' Dickie the brewer, an' Peter the skinman,
An' Geordie our deacon, for want of a better,
An' Bess, wha delights in the sins that beset her.
O, worthy St Andrew, we canna compel ye,
But ye ken as well as a body can tell ye,
If these gang to heaven, we'll a' be sae shockit,
Your garret o' blue will but thinly be stockit.

" But for a' the rest, for the women's sake, save them,
Their bodies at least, an' their sauls, if they have them ;
But it puzzles Jock Lesly, an' sma' it avails,
If they dwell in their stamocks, their heads, or their tails.
An' save, without word of confession auricular,
The clerk's bonny daughters, an' Bell in particular ;
For ye ken that their beauty's the pride an' the staple
Of the great wicked village of Balmaquhapple ! "

THE SKYLARK

Bird of the wilderness,
Blithesome and cumberless,
Sweet be thy matin o'er moorland and lea !
Emblem of happiness,
Blest is thy dwelling-place—
O to abide in the desert with thee !
Wild is thy lay and loud,
Far in the downy cloud,
Love gives it energy, love gave it birth.
Where, on thy dewy wing,
Where art thou journeying ?
Thy lay is in heaven, thy love is on earth.

O'er fell and fountain sheen,
O'er moor and mountain green,
O'er the red streamer that heralds the day,
Over the cloudlet dim,
Over the rainbow's rim,
Musical cherub, soar, singing, away !
Then, when the gloaming comes,
Low in the heather blooms
Sweet will thy welcome and bed of love be !
Emblem of happiness,
Blest is thy dwelling-place—
O to abide in the desert with thee !

A BOY'S SONG

Where the pools are bright and deep,
Where the grey trout lies asleep,
Up the river and over the lea,
That's the way for Billy and me.

Where the blackbird sings the latest,
Where the hawthorn blooms the sweetest,
Where the nestlings chirp and flee,
That's the way for Billy and me.

Where the mowers mow the cleanest,
Where the hay lies thick and greenest,
There to track the homeward bee,
That's the way for Billy and me.

Where the hazel bank is steepest,
Where the shadow falls the deepest,
Where the clustering nuts fall free,
That's the way for Billy and me.

Why the boys should drive away
Little sweet maidens from the play,
Or love to banter and fight so well,
That's the thing I never could tell.

But this I know, I love to play
Through the meadow, among the hay ;
Up the water and over the lea,
That's the way for Billy and me.

WHEN THE KYE COMES HAME

Come all ye jolly shepherds
    That whistle through the glen,
I'll tell ye of a secret
    That courtiers dinna ken :

What is the greatest bliss
  That the tongue o' man can name?
'Tis to woo a bonny lassie
  When the kye comes hame.
    When the kye comes hame,
    When the kye comes hame,
     'Tween the gloaming and the mirk,
    When the kye comes hame.

'Tis not beneath the coronet,
  Nor canopy of state,
'Tis not on couch of velvet,
  Nor arbour of the great—
'Tis beneath the spreading birk,
  In the glen without the name,
Wi' a bonny, bonny lassie,
  When the kye comes hame.
    When the kye comes hame, etc.

There the blackbird bigs his nest
  For the mate he loes to see,
And on the topmost bough,
  O, a happy bird is he ;
Where he pours his melting ditty,
  And love is a' the theme,
And he'll woo his bonny lassie
  When the kye comes hame.
    When the kye comes hame, etc.

When the blewart bears a pearl,
  And the daisy turns a pea,
And the bonny lucken gowan
  Has fauldit up her ee,
Then the laverock frae the blue lift
  Doups down, an' thinks nae shame
To woo his bonny lassie .
  When the kye comes hame.
    When the kye comes hame, etc.

See yonder pawkie shepherd,
   That lingers on the hill,
His ewes are in the fauld,
   An' his lambs are lying still ;
Yet he downa gang to bed,
   For his heart is in a flame,
To meet his bonny lassie
    When the kye comes hame.
      When the kye comes hame, etc.

When the little wee bit heart
   Rises high in the breast,
An' the little wee bit starn
   Rises red in the east,
O there's a joy sae dear,
   That the heart can hardly frame,
Wi' a bonny, bonny lassie,
    When the kye comes hame !
      When the kye comes hame, etc.

Then since all nature joins
   In this love without alloy,
O, wha wad prove a traitor
   To Nature's dearest joy ?
Or wha wad choose a crown,
   Wi' its perils and its fame,
And *miss* his bonny lassie
    When the kye comes hame ?
     When the kye comes hame,
     When the kye comes hame,
      'Tween the gloaming and the mirk,
     When the kye comes hame !

BIRNIEBOUZLE

WILL ye gang wi' me, lassie,
To the braes o' Birniebouzle?
Baith the yird an' sea, lassie,
Will I rob to fend ye.
I'll hunt the otter an' the brock,
The hart, the hare, an' heather cock,
An' pu' the limpet aff the rock,
To batten an' to mend ye.

If ye'll gang wi' me, lassie,
To the braes o' Birniebouzle,
Till the day you dee, lassie,
Want shall ne'er come near ye.
The peats I'll carry in a skull,
The cod an' ling wi' hooks I'll pull,
An' reave the eggs o' mony a gull,
To please my denty dearie.

Sae canty will we be, lassie,
At the braes o' Birniebouzle,
Donald Gunn and me, lassie,
Ever sall attend ye.
Though we hae nowther milk nor meal,
Nor lamb nor mutton, beef nor veal,
We'll fank the porpy and the seal,
And that's the way to fend ye.

An' ye sall gang sae braw, lassie,
At the kirk o' Birniebouzle,
Wi' littit brogues an' a', lassie,
Wow but ye'll be vaunty!
An' you sall wear, when you are wed,
The kirtle an' the Heeland plaid,
An' sleep upon a heather bed,
Sae cozy an' sae canty.

If ye'll but marry me, lassie,
At the kirk o' Birniebouzle,
A' my joy shall be, lassie,
Ever to content ye.
I'll bait the line and bear the pail,
An' row the boat and spread the sail,
An' drag the larry at my tail,
When mussel hives are plenty.

Then come awa wi' me, lassie,
To the braes o' Birniebouzle ;
Bonny lassie, dear lassie,
You shall ne'er repent ye.
For you shall own a bught o' ewes,
A brace o' gaits, and byre o' cows,
An' be the lady o' my house,
An' lads an' lasses plenty.

LOVE IS LIKE A DIZZINESS

I LATELY lived in quiet case
    An' never wish'd to marry, O !
But when I saw my Peggy's face,
    I felt a sad quandary, O !
Though wild as ony Athol deer,
    She has trepann'd me fairly, O !
Her cherry cheeks an' een sae clear
    Torment me late an early, O !
        O, love, love, love !
            Love is like a dizziness ;
        It winna let a poor body
            Gang about his biziness !

To tell my feats this single week
  Wad mak a daft-like diary, O !
I drave my cart outow'r a dike,
  My horses in a miry, O !
I wear my stockings white an' blue,
  My love's sae fierce an' fiery, O !
I drill the land that I should plough,
  An' plough the drills entirely, O !
    O, love, love, love ! etc.

Ae morning, by the dawn o' day,
  I rase to theek the stable, O !
I keust my coat, an' plied away
  As fast as I was able, O !
I wrought that morning out an' out,
  As I'd been redding fire, O !
When I had done an' look'd about,
  Gudefaith, it was the byre, O !
    O, love, love, love ! etc.

Her wily glance I'll ne'er forget,
  The dear, the lovely blinkin o't
Has pierced me through an' through the heart,
  An' plagues me wi' the prinkling o't.
I tried to sing, I tried to pray,
  I tried to drown't wi' drinkin' o't,
I tried wi' sport to drive't away,
  But ne'er can sleep for thinkin' o't.
    O, love, love, love ! etc.

Nae man can tell what pains I prove,
  Or how severe my pliskie, O !
I swear I'm sairer drunk wi' love
  Than ever I was wi' whisky, O !

For love has raked me fore an' aft,
    I scarce can lift a leggie, O !
I first grew dizzy, then gaed daft,
    An' soon I'll dee for Peggy, O !
      O, love, love, love !
        Love is like a dizziness
      It winna let a poor body
        Gang about his biziness !

MEG O' MARLEY

O KEN ye Meg o' Marley glen,
    The bonny blue-eed dearie ?
She's play'd the deil amang the men,
    An' a' the land's grown eery ;
She's stown the " Bangor " frae the clerk,
    An' snool'd him wi' the shame o't ;
The minister's fa'n through the text,
    An' Meg gets a' the blame o't.

The ploughman ploughs without the sock ;
    The gadman whistles sparely ;
The shepherd pines amang his flock,
    An' turns his een to Marley ;
The tailor lad's fa'n ower the bed ;
    The cobler ca's a parley ;
The weaver's neb's out through the web,
    An' a' for Meg o' Marley.

What's to be done, for our gudeman
    Is flyting late an' early ?
He rises but to curse an' ban,
    An' sits down but to ferly.
But ne'er had love a brighter lowe
    Than light his torches sparely
At the bright een an' blithesome brow
    O' bonny Meg o' Marley.

WHEN MAGGY GANGS AWAY

O WHAT will a' the lads do
　When Maggy gangs away ?
O what will a' the lads do
　When Maggy gangs away ?
There's no a heart in a' the glen
　That disna dread the day.
O what will a' the lads do
　When Maggy gangs away ?

Young Jock has ta'en the hill for't—
　A waefu' wight is he ;
Poor Harry's ta'en the bed for't,
　An' laid him down to dee ;
An' Sandy's gane unto the kirk,
　And learnin' fast to pray.
And, O, what will the lads do
　When Maggy gangs away ?

The young laird o' the Lang-Shaw
　Has drunk her health in wine ;
The priest has said—in confidence—
　The lassie was divine—
And that is mair in maiden's praise
　Than ony priest should say ;
But, O, what will the lads do
　When Maggy gangs away ?

The wailing in our green glen
　That day will quaver high,
'Twill draw the redbreast frae the wood,
　The laverock frae the sky ;
The fairies frae their beds o' dew
　Will rise an' join the lay :
An' hey ! what a day will be
　When Maggy gangs away !

THE LASS O' CARLISLE

I'LL sing ye a wee bit sang,
   A sang i' the aulden style,
It is of a bonny young lass
   Wha lived in merry Carlisle.
An' O but this lass was bonny,
   An' O but this lass was braw,
An' she had gowd in her coffers,
   An' that was best of a'.
      Sing hey, hickerty dickerty,
        Hickerty dickerty dear :
        The lass that has gowd an' beauty
          Has naething on earth to fear !

This lassie had plenty o' wooers,
   As beauty an' wealth should hae ;
This lassie she took her a man,
   An' then she could get nae mae.
This lassie had plenty o' weans,
   That keepit her hands astir ;
And then she dee'd and was buried,
   An' there was an end of her.
      Sing hey, hickerty dickerty,
        Hickerty dickerty dan,
        The best thing in life is to make
          The maist o't that we can !

GOOD NIGHT, AND JOY BE WI' YOU A'

THE year is wearing to the wane,
   An' day is fading west awa' ;
Loud raves the torrent an' the rain,
   And dark the cloud comes down the shaw ;
But let the tempest tout an' blaw
   Upon his loudest winter horn,
Good night, an' joy be wi' you a' ;
   We'll maybe meet again the morn !

Oh, we hae wandered far an wide
   O'er Scotia's hills, o'er firth an' fell,
An' mony a simple flower we've cull'd,
   An' trimm'd them wi' the heather bell !
We've ranged the dingle an' the dell,
   The hamlet an' the baron's ha' ;
Now let us take a kind farewell,—
   Good night, an' joy be wi' you a' !

Though I was wayward, you were kind,
   And sorrow'd when I went astray ;
For oh, my strains were often wild
   As winds upon a winter day.
If e'er I led you from the way,
   Forgie your Minstrel aince for a' ;
A tear fa's wi' his parting lay,—
   Good night, and joy be wi' you a' !

CONCLUSION OF " THE QUEEN'S WAKE "

Now, my loved Harp, a while farewell !
   I leave thee on the old gray thorn ;
The evening dews will mar thy swell,
   That waked to joy the cheerful morn.

Farewell, sweet soother of my woe !
   Chill blows the blast around my head ;
And louder yet that blast may blow,
   When down this weary vale I've sped.

The wreath lies on Saint Mary's shore ;
   The mountain sounds are harsh and loud ;
The lofty brows of stern Clokmore
   Are visored with the moving cloud.

But Winter's deadly hues shall fade
  On moorland bald and mountain shaw,
And soon the rainbow's lovely shade
  Sleep on the breast of Bowerhope Law ;

Then will the glowing suns of Spring,
  The genial shower and stealing dew,
Wake every forest bird to sing,
  And every mountain flower renew.

But not the rainbow's ample ring,
  That spans the glen and mountain gray,
Though fanned by western breeze's wing,
  And sunned by Summer's glowing ray,

To man decayed, can ever more
  Renew the age of love and glee !
Can ever second spring restore
  To my old mountain Harp and me !

But when the hue of softened green
  Spreads over hill and lonely lea,
And lowly primrose opes unseen
  Her virgin bosom to the bee ;

When hawthorns breathe their odours far,
  And carols hail the year's return ;
And daisy spreads her silver star
  Unheeded by the mountain burn ;

Then will I seek the aged thorn,
  The haunted wild and fairy ring,
Where oft thy erring numbers borne
  Have taught the wandering winds to sing.

GLOSSARY

A

Arles, a token payment.
Attour, over.

B

Beal, fire.
Bele-fire, bonfire.
Big, build.
Birk, birch.
Bladds, fragments.
Blewart, the Germander Speedwell.
Bothy, " a dairy house, where the Highland shepherds, or graziers, live during summer with their herds and flocks, and during that season make butter and cheese " [Pennant, *Tour in Scotland, 1769*, quoted in *S.N.D.*]
Brainzelled, stirred.
Bree, broth.
Breek-knee, breeches-knee.
Brock, badger.
Bught, fold.
Burd, an ill-begotten thing.

C

Canty, cheerful, contented.
Claught, clutched, clawed.
Cludis, clouds.
Corby, raven.
Cor-cockis, moor-cocks.
Couryng, cowering, crouching.
Crouse, elated, self-satisfied.
Cruik-shell, a pot-hook.

D

Darnit, passed secretly through.
Deide, death.
Deray, disorder, confusion.
Dinner'd, dined.
Doffrinis, the Dovre Fjeld mountain range in Norway.
Doups, dips.
Downa, is unable, or reluctant.
Dree, suffer.
Driche, doleful.

E

Ee, eye.
Ee-bree, eyebrow.
Eery, weird, uncanny; apprehensive of evil.
Eident, diligent.
Eithly, easily.
Elyed, disappeared.
Ern, eagle.
Ether, adder.

F

Fank, catch, trap.
Fauld, fold.
Fend, protect, maintain, find sustenance for.
Fere, companion, attendant.
Ferit, afraid.
Ferly, to muse, or wonder.
Fire-flauchtis, lightning-flashes.
Fluffit, tossed about.
Flyting, scolding.
Forgie, forgive.

G

Gadman, the man, or boy, who drove the horses in a plough.
Gang, go.
Gate, way, road.
Gecked, mocked.
Girn, snarl, show one's teeth.
Glair, stare (glower).
Gledgin, glancing slyly, sidelong.
Gleid, spark, flame.
Gloaming, twilight.
Gloff, fear.
Gloffis, darkest places amid surrounding darkness.
Gouk, the cuckoo; one easily fooled.
Goved, moved about, staring idly and vacantly.
Gowan, daisy.
Gowd, gold.
Gowl, a great cavity, gulf.
Gowled, yelled.
Grat, cried.
Grew, greyhound.
Gurly, surly.

H

Happed, covered (as with a coverlet).
Heather-cock, the ring-ousel.
Hern, heron.
Heuch, a deep glen.
Hindberry, wild raspberry.
Hoolet, owl.
Houf, home.
Houghed, hamstrung.
Humloke, hemlock.

I

Ilka, every.
Ingle, hearth, fireplace.

J

Joup, short skirt, petticoat.

K

Kemed, combed.
Ken, know.
Kerlyngs, witches, hogs.
Keust, cast off.
Kye, cows.
Kyth, appear, show themselves.

L

Laibies, skirts or tails of a coat.
Laverock, lark.
Law, an isolated hill, or mound.
Leal, loyal.
Leifu', kindly, compassionate.
Leil, loyal.
Leme, gleam, glow.
Lened, rested.
Lickit, beat.
Lift, sky.
Liftis, sky's.
Lingel, to bind with shoemaker's thread.
Littand, causing to blush (?).
Littit, dyed.
Lowe, flame.
Lowner, calmer, lower.
Lucken, folded up.
Lug, ear.
Lum, chimney.
Lythlye, softly, easily.

M

Maike, mate, companion.
Maisry, Marjory.
Marled, chequered.
Maun, must.
Mavis, song-thrush.
Merkist, darkest.
Merl, blackbird.
Met, may.
Minny, mother.
Mirds, flattery.
Mirk, darkness.
Moon-fern, moonwort.
Moory, heathery.
Mooted, moulted, clipped.

Mouldy, earthy.
Mumpit, fooled, beguiled.
Mussel hives, mussel-beds.

N

Naigis, nags.
Neb, nose, the point of anything.
Needilit, pierced, as with a needle.
Nickering, squawking.

O

Outower, beyond.

P

Pang, strong.
Pawkie, sly.
Philabeg, kilt.
Pliskie, plight.
Ploy, frolic.
Porpy, porpoise.
Pree, taste.
Prigging, bargaining.
Prinkling, tingling.

Q

Quhill, till.

R

Raike, wander, roam ; wandering.
Reave, plunder.
Redding, putting in order.
Reif, plunder.

S

Scadd, scald.
Schaw, stalk.
Sey, essay, try.
Seymar, a loose upper garment.
Shaw, grove.
Shaw, " a piece of ground which becomes suddenly flat at the bottom of a hill or steep bank " (Jam.).
Shill, shrill.
Skull, wicker basket.
Slee, sly.

Snool'd, subdued, dispirited, shamed.
Sock, ploughshare.
Sough, a sighing sound.
Soupit, swept.
Speer, ask.
Speil, climb.
Stang'd, stung.
Starn, star.
Stown, stolen.
Swa'd (or *Swawed*), rolled along.
Swaipin, sweeping.
Swale, swelling wave.

T

Theek, thatch.
Tikes, dogs (of a rough, coarse type).
Till, to.
Tinchel, a circle of beaters.
Tod, fox.
Tove, swirled up.
Tuzzlit, tumbled about.

U

Unmeled, not tampered with, innocent.

W

Waik, a clearing (?)
Wained, conveyed.
Warlock, wizard.
Wauffing, waving.
Wawlyng, wildly rolling.
Weigh-bauk, the beam of a balance.
Wene, dwelling.
Werde, fate.
Whittle, knife.
Won, dwell.
Worst-faured, most ill-favoured.

Y

Yerk, to bind ; to jerk, or tug. [The Yerkin is " the seam by which the hinder part of the upper leather of a shoe is joined to the forepart " (Jam.)].
Yorlin, yellow-hammer.
Yout, roar, bellow.

INDEX OF TITLES AND FIRST LINES

First lines in italics